FROM
Leadership
TO
Legacy

11 Strategies to Build Connection With Your Team & Create Massive Impact

Marsha Flemmings © 2021

All rights reserved. No part of this book may be reproduced, stored, or transmitted by any means- whether auditory, graphic, mechanical, or electronic- without written permission of both publisher and author, except in the case of brief excerpts used in critical articles and certain other noncommercial uses permitted by copyright law. Unauthorized reproduction of any part of this work is illegal and punishable by law.

ISBN-13: 978-0-578-30681-0

Cover Design: Damascus Media Inc

Editor: Sammarko lightbourne

For more information, please visit:

www.marshaflemmings.com

store.marshaflemmings.com

https://linktr.ee/marshaflemmings

Table of Contents

Introduction 1

Vision 7

    Your Leadership Identity 9

    Why You Are There In The First Place 17

    What Do You See For Them? 21

Self Awareness 27

    Save You From Yourself 29

    Do You See Yourself 39

Communication 49

    What You Say 51

    When You Say 57

    How You Say 61

Connection 67

    Invest 69

Support	77
Challenge	83
Epilogue	**87**

Introduction

I am so thankful that you decided to take this walk with me by purchasing this book. My prayer is that in these pages you will come into a greater awareness of just how critical it is that as a leader you lead in a way that creates trust within your team. Not simply in your title, but in YOU. I pray you recognise that pouring all you know into your team and really helping them see themselves more clearly and helping them develop the untapped potential inside them will reap more rewards, not just for them, but for you and ultimately your organisation.

I believe that in large corporations, in small businesses, in ministry and in our homes there is an opportunity for leaders to build stronger connections, create greater impact for their people and build lasting legacy. The challenge often exists that leaders don't understand the value in doing this.

You may be frustrated because you are passionate about the work you do and truly desire to do a good job and lead well, but for some reason your team doesn't seem to see the vision with you.

From Leadership to Legacy

They may not be sharing ideas with you and you just don't understand why. You may also find that they aren't communicating openly with you and seem to do just enough to get it done. They don't seem to possess the same passion you do for meeting the goals. Or you may find that there is a crisis situation and they just don't seem to be flexible or willing to help resolve the issues. So you are stuck wondering what you can do to help your team become more engaged and passionate.

I want you to know that you are absolutely able to turn your work environment and results around. Now if you are the type of leader that thinks you know it all, that what you say goes, and whatever their issues are they need to fix them because you only care that they produce the results, then this book is not for you. However, if you truly desire to tap into the hearts of your people, inspire them, help them see and know that there is more in them and help them pull that more out, then you and I are going on this amazing journey together.

I've had the good fortune since working summer jobs and internships in my teenage years, to be led by some pretty incredible human beings. I've also had the fortune of working for and being led by some human beings that could stand to learn a bit more about leadership, emotional intelligence, and a bit more about humanity. Now before anybody comes for me, let me also acknowledge that in the lives of some I may have been

Introduction

the leader who could have learned to lead better. Thankfully in the lives of many, I've been the leader that has helped them see all that was inside them and made a huge impact in their career and lives.

I can't say what has specifically created my passion for the opportunity that leaders have to impact lives, but what I do know is that I have lived and seen the benefits of leaders who have fully embraced that opportunity. I have helped to completely shift lives, build confidence, help others see capabilities in themselves that they didn't see before and all of that positive change resulted in team members who were now totally committed to the vision I had because they trusted me. Their willingness to truly follow my lead had far more to do with who I was, the integrity with which I operated, my willingness to be transparent, my downright insistence on developing their individual and collective zone of genius, and always challenging them about what's next after they have mastered an area or skill.

This kind of approach has allowed me to help team members who were on the verge of being released from employment to winning the top awards in the company. It has also helped me guide many to multiple promotions and tapping into and also operating in work they were made to do.

I will never forget back in 2014 when I received a call while at work from one of my closest friends who worked at the corporate office of the company we were both employed to. It was unusual for her to call me that hour of the day so my mind automatically assumed that something was wrong. When I answered and I heard her say my name and do a quiet scream, I was chuckling too. But then I wondered if this was the appropriate response and I had to ask her what was going on.

What she said next moved me to tears. She said, "I am so proud of you. I am so proud of you. I've always known this about you but I want to remind you I am so proud of you." She went on to explain that they were doing panel reviews and interviews for each team member that was a part of a company-wide employee recognition program. The company, at that time, had 22 locations. Each location had a monthly procedure that led to an annual selection for the top awards, one of which identified a single team member that was recognised as the team member of the year. They were hosting those 22 team members and preparing to cater the fanciest awards ceremony where one of those contenders would be selected as the ultimate team member company-wide.

I knew that the event would be happening soon, so hearing her I figured the team member from my location may have said something complimentary, but what she said exceeded my expectation. She spoke of a team member that worked with me at a location I had been promoted from 4 years prior. She

Introduction

explained, " the way he spoke about you, what you instilled in him and the rest of the team, how you believed in him, saw more in him than he imagined was inside himself was remarkable. You have been gone from there for 4 years and you should hear him speak of the impact you made on him and the rest of the team there." I shed tears for real then.

Being given a glimpse into the difference I made in my team's life and career was not new to me, but each time I heard it, it further solidified that I was most fueled by helping others see, tap into, and live every ounce of greatness they had in them. To have been gone from that location for 4 years, to know the caliber of managers that the team had access to, I was just grateful that my impact went from leadership to legacy. How? I saw something in him that he didn't see in himself. I helped him see it. I challenged him to tap into it and live it and it changed his career and who he was would never be the same.

He wasn't the first and after him there were many more. I only know this for a fact by their own admission. So I'm not trying to drink my own Kool-Aid or sell it to you.

For this very reason, I wanted to share what I learned that allowed me to make this kind of impact, over and over for two decades. All too often I've observed leaders that are so focused on the task, the numbers, the operation, and "all the things". Meanwhile, they are overlooking and undervaluing the very

From Leadership to Legacy

resource that can impact everything else in the organisation. It is my desire, through this book, to help as many that will read to actually step up, lead and live beyond a title and make a real commitment to move from leadership to legacy.

Vision

Your Leadership Identity

(Vision For Yourself)

I am tomorrow, or some future day, what I establish today. I am today what I established yesterday or some previous day.

James Joyce

One of the mistakes a lot of people make is looking for lessons of who to be and completely overlooking the lessons of who not to be. I once had a general manager who spoke with such conviction about a manager that he had as a young professional in hospitality. He would tell us of this manager's lack of patience, lack of organisational skills, and lack of respect. Honestly, his manager just sounded like a terrible person to work with and for, but one of the things he was always mindful to say is that he looked at that manager and made up his mind that whenever he became a leadership he would never be like him.

From Leadership to Legacy

He was on to something. First he had the good sense to think ahead and to determine when he became a leader what he wanted to stand for and also what he did not want to represent. Unfortunately, not very many people do this. Yes, a lot of people envision the path their career will take, the promotions they desire to achieve, and that ultimate dream job. Far too few give the same thought and energy to who they want to be in those roles, how they want to impact not just the organisational goals, but the teams that will support them in achieving those goals.

One of the first things I want to propose that you do as an emerging leader or if you are already in leadership and recognise that your connection and ability to influence and impact your team is not what it could be, is determine now who you want to be as a leader. Do you envision that you are the kind of leader that:

- Listens well?
- Is trusted by your team?
- Is not making success only about you?
- Challenges your team so they can grow?
- Sets a healthy standard for communication?
- Handles setbacks in a constructive way?

Your Leadership Identity

- Leads well through change?
- Sees & nurtures the potential within your team?
- Is confident in your own abilities?
- Is confident in the abilities of your team?
- Whose opinion and vision are valued?
- Allows your team to function in their zone of genius?
- Is not threatened by the potential in others?
- Has a vision for your growth?

You want to establish from the very beginning, or at minimum from this point moving forward, who you want to be as a leader. By doing this you are establishing a set of criteria, a standard for which you will hold yourself accountable because the truth is like any other goal in life, if we are unclear about how we want to show up, we are going to show up any old way as Jamaicans would say and reap any old results.

So here's the thing. Let's say you decide you want to get healthier and fitter. Typically what we do is decide to drop 20 pounds. We decide we'd like to see some definition in our arms and abs or in our legs and we really start to specify what we want to see. We really start to specify the end result. We even pick out an outfit that we want to be able to fit into when we get to the point where we are satisfied. I am simply proposing that we take the same approach to leadership. Take an opportunity to establish that this is the type of leader that I would like to be. This is how I would like to engage my team. This is how I would like to impact them. This is the type of result that I want to create. These are the ways that I want to see my team perform as a result of my leadership. So what do we do next when we want to lose weight, when we decide we want to fit into a particular outfit, when we decide we want to drop x amount of pounds, and when we decide we want to see the definition of the muscles in our arms and abs and legs? We have the end goal in mind and now we have to determine how we get there. Our approach to leadership should not be any different.

I remember when I was just starting out in the company that I worked for 19 years. I was a young girl walking into a new industry. I was walking into a new job with a new team. I was not going to be the manager or leader for the department, I was simply one of the team members. Before getting even a minute of training what I knew was that I wanted to show up focused. I wanted to become absolutely clear on what my job was and I wanted to be exceptional. I wanted to make sure that I was contributing strongly to the team and that I was giving my best self every single day.

Your Leadership Identity

As a result of that awareness I decided that when we were going through training I would not allow anything to distract me. I was going to ensure that I asked questions. I was going to ensure that I showed up everyday with a disposition or a posture that says I'm ready to get to work.

When I started the entire team for that department was new. We all started at the same time with the exception of the manager who had started two months before us. Within a week of starting and completing orientation, all of the team members were sent to a second location to do some hands-on training experience. The day we were preparing to depart by bus, the manager came to me and she pulled me aside, informing me that I have the responsibility of making sure that everyone conducts themselves properly, shows up on time and is representing the company well.

This caught me by surprise. I had no indication before that moment what would cause her to have that confidence in me. All of us that were going were equal team members. We were all new. We were all learning the same information at the same time and I just didn't quite get at the time why I was handpicked for that responsibility. Years later I would come to find out. In conversation one day, the manager made it clear. She said, "you showed up on the very first day and it was clear you were taking your job seriously. It was clear that you meant to do your best.

From Leadership to Legacy

It was obvious you were intentional to present yourself well and the organisation well. It was clear that you knew how to communicate with others not just professionally, but that you knew how to somehow influence people to want to do the same."

See, this job had come 9 months after being fired from a job I was doing extremely well in. You may have read about that in my first book. Those 9 months were some of the toughest of my life up until that point. There was not a whole lot that made me feel like a failure back then. Sure, I never felt like I "fit in" many places, but feeling like a failure was not commonplace for me. Those nine months wrecked me.

So walking into this new opportunity, I got very clear and said, "Marsha, when you walk on to this new job you are going to give your best effort. You are going to apply yourself. You are going to learn all that you can. You are going to show up every single day representing yourself in a way that makes you proud. I had no idea that was going to cause leaders or anyone in the organisation to notice me.

The thing that I really want you to connect with and understand is that who you are as a leader, how you show up, how you impact the people around you, how you impact your team, your ability to influence them, and their willingness to allow you to influence them is going to be directly connected to who you are. It is tied to how you show up and how you engage them because

Your Leadership Identity

people will not allow you to influence them if they do not trust you.

So here is where I want you to take a moment and become clear on the vision that you have about your leadership:

- Do you think that your leadership is all about you?
- Do you think that your voice as a leader is the only voice that matters?
- Do you think you need to do it all yourself because you are the only one who can do it right?
- What is your view on how communication flows to and from you as a leader?
- What is your view on how you will handle your own mistakes?
- Will you own your mistakes?
- Will you play the blame game?
- How do you view your responsibility to your team?
- How will you equip them?
- How will you train them or will you groom them?
- How will you support them?

From Leadership to Legacy

- How will you invest in them?
- How will you promote them?
- What are the principles that you will be standing on?
- Do you believe in transparency?
- What do you believe about maintaining an image?
- Do you believe in equipping and empowering your people to make decisions to get the job done?
- Or do you believe that everything must come through you?

Why You Are There In The First Place

(Vision For organisational Goals)

Leadership is the capacity to translate vision into reality.

Warren G. Bennis.

I'll cut to the chase here because I know there are a lot of you already looking at me sideways. Not everyone walks into their job or their career, despite their ambitions, with a true vision for how they will own the organisational goals and how they along with their teams will execute to achieve them.

I get it. Truly I do. No one in the organisation would be there if it did not exist, and the organisation exists to accomplish very specific things. Whether you are the boss-lady-in-chief of your own operation or you are one of the head boss ladies in someone else's organisation, the fact is, you have a set of goals that you need to accomplish and you've either hired or been given a team to do it with.

While this book has a strong focus on how you connect with your team, groom and invest in them, it is still very clear that you cannot lose sight of what you've been hired to accomplish, or if it's your own organisation, what you started your business to accomplish.

What does it mean to have a vision for the organisational goals and a strategy for how you and your team will achieve them?

It is crucial that you as the leader are crystal clear on what the company is created to achieve. You also need to be clear on the principles that the organisation is meant to stand on to accomplish those goals. Without that clarity for yourself it will be impossible to guide your team to success because to lead you have to be taking them somewhere. You, more than anyone else, must know where that somewhere is.

At a few different points in my career I was either part of a team leading the expansion of a location or single-handedly launching a new department when the model was changed in one of our locations. In each instance, a critical part of the process was not just handling recruiting, but also training these new recruits on the job they were being hired to do and teaching them the values the organisation was built on that governed how we treated each

Why You Are There In The First Place

other and how we treated clients.

Take any role in an organisation. You can hire and train someone on the specific tasks they have to perform. A leader is going to go far beyond that. Why? A leader knows that for success to happen, anyone on the team has to go beyond simply being able to complete tasks on a list. A leader knows that success will require a team to fully grasp the values of an organisation and also buy into those values. Further, a leader is going to consistently demonstrate those values to the team and clients.

Having a vision for achieving organisational objectives will require you as a leader to determine what kind of synergy needs to exist, how to cultivate it, how you will position the people on your team to be able to capitalise on each person's strengths and a host of other components that go beyond their technical skills.

As I reflect on my career in hospitality, the team that I consider to be among the best I experienced, if not the team I led most successfully, was a team that I made sure to do a few things with:

- They were thoroughly trained in their technical areas.

- They were consistently and thoroughly trained in the organisation's standard of service delivery and were often challenged on how they could go beyond.

- Always facilitated discussions about the vision and mission of the company and how it influenced the different decisions that were being made.

- We frequently examined their own vision for themselves and how that aligned with the organisation.

- Always presented a challenge for how we can continue to grow after achieving targets.

- Trained 100% of the team to be multifunctional.

- Helped them see their role in the organisation as critical.

What Do You See For Them?

(Vision For Your Team)

"Before you are a leader, success is all about growing yourself. When you become a leader, success is all about growing others."

Jack Welch

There was once a young man who had applied to work on my team. Let's call him Cedric. Cedric was already a part of the organisation, but worked in another department on another manager's team. During his interview, I probed him about his performance in his current department and I also asked about his response to his leadership team in that area. What quickly became evident was that Cedric was not so much motivated by a desire or passion to be on my team or even passionate about the work that we did in that area. What was in fact more evident was his strong desire to no longer be a part of the team that he was on.

From Leadership to Legacy

During an interview there are several things that I look for and usually I prefer to hire someone who at minimum has an interest in the area they're applying for. However, after having a conversation with Cedric's existing leader, and also acknowledging the evidence of Cedric's frustration, I still decided to take a chance on him.

I decided to take a chance on him because in our conversation I **saw something in him that I knew our team could benefit from and I believed I could help him cultivate it.** Within 3 years of joining my team, not only was he excelling, he had received a promotion within the first 2 years and went on to beat out over 600 other employees and earned the top award that year.

In a conversation years later, he expressed his gratitude. He explained that he knew his interview with me was not his best. He also acknowledged that he was in fact very frustrated and agitated in his previous role and had his own set of concerns. He became a bit emotional expressing how thankful he was that I saw more in him than what he showed me at the time. He confessed that since joining my team, I always challenged him to not settle with each accomplishment, but kept asking him "what's next" and that helped him to create and clarify his own vision.

I believe that since you are reading this book you are already

What Do You See For Them?

someone who knows that leadership is so much more than the title you hold. It is more than having and wielding power and getting to call the shots. If no one is following you, I'm sorry to tell you that you are not leading. What will cause people to follow you? They are going to follow you because they connect with you. They connect with something in you. They connect with how they feel in your presence. They also will be willing to follow when they trust you and trust your vision. Not just your vision for the company, but your vision for them and how they will benefit.

So when leading, ask yourself, are you seeing the people on your team? Have you created a vision for them as a unit? Have you created a vision for how you want your team to execute? How do you organise and strategize based on their collective & individual strengths? How do you envision helping them build? How do you envision helping them grow as professionals and people?

The fact that you are in an organisation and you are in a role where you are assigned direct oversight for a group of people does not automatically mean they will follow you. Without connection and their trust you may find that they really just show up and do what is required and what needs to be done. You may have a few exceptional ones who are so self-driven that despite any lack of leadership they show up with more desire to learn, produce, and grow because they are already clear on their own vision.

However, what really creates a true opportunity for people to give you their trust, buy into your vision and follow your lead is when they recognise that you don't just see them as a number in the organisation, you see THEM. When they believe that you see them, you see their potential, capability and capacity and you are also committed to helping them grow those things, maximise those things and help take them to another level, then you have really started to tap into where the magic happens.

Yes, we get it. No one would be in that job in that company if that organisation didn't have a set of objectives they needed to achieve. One of the ways you ensure you are not driving yourself crazy trying to do all things, be all things, know all things, and figure out all things is by having a clear vision of the kind of team you can support in accomplishing those goals.

Each member on your team has a zone of genius, most won't even know it yet. When you can map out the way that you can guide them to achieve and then exceed the company targets, while helping them identify, operate in and expand their zone of genius they become unstoppable and you become the leader who becomes known for taking everything and everyone you touch to the next level.

What Do You See For Them?

Let's take the example of Cedric from the opening of this chapter. I decided to hire Cedric despite his poor interview because I already had a vision for my team. I already recognised where we had some holes affecting our ability to accomplish that vision, not just in the manning, but also in the kind of people we needed to add to the team to accomplish what we were working towards. I was able to identify that some of what we needed was in him despite his inability to put his best foot forward.

Sure I could have walked into interviews looking solely for the technical skills a person has to be able to execute the job, but that's not all I needed and as a leader that is not all you will need when you are building your team. But you first have to know what you are building in order to be able to identify what's missing and who is needed.

Become clear on:

- What kind of team are you building?
- How do they operate?
- How do they communicate?
- At what rate are they growing?
- How do they execute?

- What do you want them to achieve that goes beyond the organisational goals?

- What mindset do they have?

- What attitude do they bring?

- What synergy exists?

- What skills are needed for this team to be effective?

Becoming clear on these things will guide your recruitment process and decisions. It will guide how you train, how you equip, how you invest, support, challenge, delegate, and plan. Without this kind of clarity and forward thinking about the kind of team you are building, you will inevitably recruit based on technical skills only. Success for new team members, the organisation, and for you is going to require so much more than that.

Self Awareness

Save You From Yourself

Many leadership problems are driven by low self awareness.

Bill Hybels

One of the most disruptive, toxic, unproductive, and damaging traits that a leader could possess is a lack of self-awareness. I have seen it over and over and over in my career. Looking back at my own career particularly when I was much younger, I can see where my lack of awareness impacted my ability to lead well.

I recall very vividly hosting a disciplinary meeting with a young lady who was on my team. She had been involved in a matter that had arisen on the job. After meeting with all the parties involved and after doing a thorough investigation using the camera footage from the surveillance that was available, we determined very clearly the role she played in the matter. We had a few preliminary meetings with the different parties involved and as we got to the end of the decision-making process in terms of holding each party accountable, we scheduled a meeting with her on this particular day. The meeting would be with her, my then assistant and me. When we entered the meeting, we knew we would be discussing the findings of the investigation and how we would be holding her accountable for her role in what happened.

On the scheduled day, my assistant and I met with her to communicate how she would be held accountable for her actions in the entire matter. The meeting commenced and as I had anticipated she was very quiet, seemingly pensive, and her body language and facial expressions suggested that she was not anticipating a positive outcome for herself. My assistant and I took the liberty of reviewing the facts of what transpired. These facts were confirmed by her. We discussed not only how her actions were damaging and in breach of company policy, but also allowed her the opportunity to indicate how she could have handled the matter differently. This confirmed that she was clear on how she should have handled the matter based on protocol.

We then discussed the different courses of action that the company allowed us as the leaders to take and ultimately the decision we were making. She had been given the most lenient decision allowed based on multiple considerations. I explained the document that was prepared and detailed what it spoke to, which in essence was an outline of what transpired, the company's position on such actions, and ultimately management's decision.

I handed her the document to review, advised her to query it if necessary, and then sign it. I observed her as she read through the document, prepared to sign it, and then stopped. Suddenly she realized that she had something to say. She crossed her arms on her lap and said that she thought the decision I was making was very hypocritical. Pump the brakes! All my life knowing myself, these were fighting words to me. Don't judge me. I'm just being honest.

She immediately went on to explain that she couldn't wrap her mind around a manager who could be so encouraging when she is doing well, who even encourages her professional endeavours outside of the organisation, but would find it necessary to have meetings with her when "something would happen" or if a mistake was made. It was just outright hypocrisy in her eyes.

Now, all of that took her maybe a minute to express. At about 25 seconds I was doing an internal check in because, well, I know me. Integrity is a huge deal to me. It is something that I worked on with great focus and effort for years to ensure that I was as integrous as I am and was even in the season we were having that encounter. So when faced with an accusation of that nature that carried a lot of weight for me. So my check-in went something like this in my head.

"Hold up. What? Hypocrite? Oh. But Marsha, your heart isn't racing. There is no heat coming from your ears and a bunch of expletives aren't swimming in your head."

Again! Do not judge me. I had not yet started living for God…so yeah…I absolutely had those thoughts and uttered them in the privacy of my confidential spaces. However, in exactly 2.5 seconds flat I recognised that I wasn't triggered and I gave myself a little mental pat on the back and refocused on her. I was truly proud of myself.

I allowed her to continue to express her interpretation of being held accountable for her actions. Even greater, I was able to really hear her and recognise that this was not an attempt to be rude, but in her own way of thinking, she genuinely could not understand the accountability she was facing.

After she had stopped speaking, I assured her that I heard her and that I understood the way she was looking at the situation. Before going any further I asked her to confirm or deny a few things:

1. Did the situation happen as you stated it and as the investigation proved? Yes.
2. Were these your actions in the matter? Yes.
3. Does the company policy speak to this matter? Yes.

4. Does the decision fall within the guidelines outlined in the employee handbook? Yes

5. Does the policy allow for an even more severe measure of accountability? Yes.

6. By your own admission are these the things you could have and should have done differently? Yes.

Now for someone who is reading this thinking that you would not have the time to go through all of that, your decision is your decision and too bad for anyone who has an issue with it, then you are one of the very people I hope this book helps. My line of questioning was to accomplish a few things, but above most of those things was to facilitate her understanding & learning so as to avoid that mistake in the future.

What does it matter if I make a decision, hold her accountable and she walks away without me ever having made an attempt to get her to step outside of what her emotions were allowing her to see and to really learn and grow from the situation.

At the end of her responding to those questions, she signed the document. I also took the opportunity to let her know I heard her. I really heard her and could see very clearly what her perspective was. I respected her right to that perspective and not only did I see it differently, I saw it more accurately. I didn't see it accurately because I had the decision making power in that situation. I just understood what my function was in my role and by her answering the questions, it alerted me to the fact that on some level she also got it.

I explained that I truly believed that as she continued to grow professionally and in her entrepreneurial efforts she would gain greater understanding of the role of a leader. I further explained that I believed she would grow to understand that the functions and responsibilities of a leader absolutely include encouraging and acknowledging a job well done and they also include correcting when poor decisions or mistakes are made. They also include establishing where things went wrong and how when faced with a similar situation again, how it should be handled. I told her support is not just a pat on the back and singing praises. Support also includes tough conversations and without them we don't grow.

I share this story because I want to point out that as the leader, if I had not already been working on self awareness I would have mishandled a teachable moment and I would not have led with grace. I would have set a poor example of what leadership looked like and while it is not in my character to just absolutely lose all my good sense, I could have reacted badly simply because I wasn't aware enough to know my triggers and how to combat them.

My quick self check-in was me making sure that I wasn't having a negative response internally that could somehow manifest itself externally.

Our self awareness exposes blindspots and gives us an opportunity to maneuver them successfully. While my story may point to my awareness of my emotional triggers, self awareness really has to do with every single aspect of who we are. It is your conscious knowledge of yourself, what drives you, what inspires you, what triggers, drains or frustrates you, and how you respond to those things. It is important because our natural responses to these things don't automatically mean it is best for us, healthy for us or helpful in allowing us to produce the results we want to produce in the spaces we occupy.

I'm sorry for any grown person who intentionally holds on to the belief that "this is just how I am" and sees that "just how you are" is affecting your leadership, your success or your growth and you refuse to improve that, is just crazy to me. Don't get me wrong, I know it takes work. I know it's not often easy.

You are talking to a woman who at the age of 23 was thrown into one of the most difficult leadership circumstances I have faced in my life with virtually no formal leadership development, except what life had given to me. In a new country managing over 120 full time staff and over 30 casual workers, of about 6 different nationalities, in a country where expatriates were not warmly welcomed, especially those from my country, and in a department that was having some devastating results in some critical areas that affected the company's bottom line. Oh! Did I mention that at least two persons there already thought they should have the position that I was promoted into?

Did I mention I didn't apply for the job?

Did I mention I didn't know anything about this country or its people until I was told about the promotion?

Did I mention my first day walking in I said good morning, a group of the supervisors who would be reporting to me did not even as much as look in my direction, let alone respond?

Did I say I was only 23? Or that I was from a small family and my dad taught me to respect everyone and that I didn't understand the concept of disliking someone simply because they were born in a different country?

I mean call me sheltered, but I just didn't get it. But I was that girl thrown into that situation, one day dealing with a woman on my team who sat in a meeting and blatantly lied. I mean fixed her mouth and uttered words that never happened and when I tell you I cried…I mean hyperventilated and excused myself from life that day.

Aside from my obvious embarrassment, I vowed that I needed to figure out how to never let myself lay so exposed emotionally on my job again. I was a mess and it took me years to not be as hot a mess. So believe me when I say I get that it takes work to see ourselves and effectively work to improve, create lasting change or simply manage how we respond to the world around us.

However it is crucial. If we are to produce the results we desire to produce for ourselves, our teams and organisations we need to learn how we respond to all these different factors, what responses hurt or help our chances of success and how we can successfully manage the responses that hurt our chances and build the behaviours that help us.

It really is a matter of what you want to accomplish and if you are willing to get out of your own way.

Do You See Yourself

"Self-awareness gives you the capacity to learn from your mistakes as well as your successes. It enables you to keep growing."

Lawrence Bossidy

There are so many layers to discover about self awareness but, there first needs to be a willingness to see yourself. There needs to be a willingness to acknowledge the toxic, the beneficial, the productive and the unproductive traits, responses, and behaviours you exhibit. Without the willingness to see it, address it and improve it, just know that the results you produce in any area of your life, not just in the spaces you lead, will not be nearly what it could and should be.

Can we just revisit the young lady I worked with that called me a hypocrite really quickly?

What prepared me for a moment like that? What allowed me to be able to respond and not react? What allowed me to be able to handle the moment in a way that demonstrated to the team member who was having a concern that communicating a thought that may be tough for the leader to hear, doesn't somehow impact their position or value on the team?

I was prepared because years before, I started having the awareness that the things I desired to accomplish in my life, with my team, and in my career were going to be directly impacted by me. My success is going to not only be influenced by me engaging in life but how I engage with life. While I took way too long working to build any one area, I actively worked on self examination and assessing what I was doing and what ways I was responding that supported me in achieving those things and those things that would likely hold me back.

Whether you are leading your own company, are a leader in someone else's organisation, in ministry, or in your home, there is a level of influence that people allow you to have only when they trust you, trust your intentions, and your capabilities. Your ability to recognise the behaviours and responses that influence building or demolishing that trust is a foundation of creating success.

During my experience I had a colleague who came to me most frustrated one day. He was also a leader within the organisation. To put some context to this, we were located on a very small island in the Caribbean, with a very small workforce. The workforce was so small that the organisation perpetually struggled to be able to operate with the full manning allowance. The country had a pretty strict approach impacting the extent to which companies could recruit expatriates and the locals living on different islands did not seem motivated to relocate for employment to the island we operated on. These conditions presented a unique set of challenges for leaders in organisations.

When my colleague came to me he explained that he wanted my perspective on a situation he was handling. A team member of his came to him during the peak of service time and asked to be excused to go pay her utility bill. Again, we are on a remote island, so though you may be wondering why in 2010 she didn't just hop online and get it handled, let's just say it is a bit indicative of how remote we were.

He said his team member explained that if she didn't leave to pay the bill her electricity would be disconnected by the end of day. His answer to her was simply no. She stood stunned looking at him, he explained and he repeated his response. She left without a word. She returned to her area and in a short while he started getting complaints from clients about her service and attitude.

After walking to her area, he quickly observed that her anger and frustration were extremely evident in her face, her body language, and in her tone of voice. Guess who suffered? The clients.

He was asking me because we had a rapport that allowed us to openly discuss the differences in our approach in leading our teams. So his question to me was simply if he was wrong. I provided my take on the matter. Let's be clear. She obviously had to be held accountable for her actions, but I took the liberty of explaining how I would have handled the situation differently.

My approach didn't involve her happily skipping off to handle her personal matters and leaving our operation in disaster. However, it included me extending options to her and some kind of support. He listened intently but the smirk coming across his face already started to communicate to me before he opened his mouth again. He then exclaimed, "but why should I have to go through all of that? I hire grown people. I don't hire children. It is not my responsibility to now help them manage their personal lives!!!!" He was so passionate that I felt that if ever he was a man prone to tears, he would have burst into it right then and there.

The conversation that ensued between us spoke to the fact that it isn't his responsibility to manage the personal lives of his team and the truth is that the age range, experience, exposure, and size of the workforce available presented a set of challenges that were not very common.

Do You See Yourself

I was very clear on my position against how she responded. However I also urged him to consider some of the abiding mindsets that as leaders in that environment we would have to be committed to work on improving or forever be fighting against things we could help them overcome. I understood that this kind of request wasn't the normal experience with her. I thought that while helping her manage her personal life wasn't a part of his job description, he missed an opportunity to offer her something other than no.

We spoke at length about it because his proclivities in leadership were in direct opposition to mine and while I knew that, I tried to help him consider a different perspective than his own.

Again, one of the challenges we had in that particular location was frequently not having the full complement of the manning. There were always opportunities for team members in all, if not most departments, to earn overtime weekly. Many managers got people on their team to not just sign up for overtime hours or agree to work overtime hours, but also to request overtime hours. So as I had a thought I asked him a question. I asked him how easily he was able to get persons to come in to work extra hours when he had someone call out from work. No surprise to me, it was a struggle for him. His exact response was, " Almost never. Almost never able to get anyone to stay extra hours or to come in to pick up an extra shift."

This for me was very telling. We were in the first year of operation in that location as a company. We were the major employer on the island with a population of about 10, 000 at the time. Due to my role I had access to information that allowed me to know that many managers were able to get their teams to take on additional hours. He was having a very different experience. When I queried with him why he thought he had such difficulty, his response was that his team didn't want money.

I want you to stick with that for a second. THEY. DIDN'T. WANT. MONEY.

Please understand, I completely get it. I completely agree and know that there are teams that are not motivated by money. However, in this particular instance in an environment with a new company that already at opening was the major employer on an island that had seen the departure of a major employer at least a year before, and in an environment where most if not all departments had persons who were willing and requesting additional hours, he concluded that his team did not want money.

Over time and with continued conversations with some of the varied challenges he would discuss with me, I recognised that he just was not seeing himself. He was not seeing the ripple effects of his actions.

Do You See Yourself

We all understand that people can respond to you based on the position you hold. We know it as positional power, which if you ask me, is really powerless. However, when people respond to you because of who you are, then you are tapping into leadership. If who you are is influencing no one in the direction of the goal and vision you have then you are simply not leading.

He was missing the evidence that pointed to his team, not one, not two, not three persons, but the great majority of his team did not trust him to influence them. Based on what he shared, I deduced that it was in large part due to them believing that he didn't care about them as individuals. He was concerned about them showing up and doing what needed to be done and him doing the same.

Please understand this, we all ultimately have a responsibility to show up and do what we are required to do. I want to highlight though that who we are showing up as in our capacity as leaders ultimately affects the work that our team gets done, how well they get it done, and what success that leads to. I really believe that it is irresponsible to think that how you communicate, handle conflict, changes, challenges, setbacks, and successes doesn't communicate to and impact your team. I believe it is even more irresponsible to expect that how you engage with your team in those circumstances doesn't impact your team and ultimately the success of the team.

So take a moment now and reflect on these questions. I would love to say that no one will know the answer but you. Truth is, if ever your team is given these questions about you, it is highly likely they can answer with a great degree of accuracy as they are observing you.

- Do I believe that leadership requires me to invest in my team?
- How am I demonstrating this belief in my actions?
- Does this belief support success for my team?
- How do I handle setbacks?
- What do I believe that communicates to my team about me?
- What do I believe that communicates to my team about how they should handle setbacks?
- Do I blame my team for setbacks?
- Do I lose my cool?
- How has this affected success?
- What frustrates me at work?
- How do I handle it?

Do You See Yourself

- Is my response to my frustrations helping to create success for myself and for my team?

- How can I handle it in a way that supports success?

- How do I approach my written communication when triggered?

- Does that approach support my success and growth?

- How do I approach my verbal communication?

- Does that approach support my success and growth?

- How do I treat my team generally?

- Does that support the success of the team?

- Does that support my success as a leader?

Communication

What You Say

Effectively clear communication is crucial to a transformational leadership while poor communication is it's biggest enemy.

Farshad Asl

There is a huge responsibility that we have as leaders as it relates to communication. The first part that we are going to dissect is what you say. This is meant to take us beyond information that is shared for the purpose of learning. This is meant to take us beyond information that is shared for the purpose of strategy development far from goal setting. I am talking about communicating as a leader in difficult times or times of success, and taking complete ownership of what we say.

One year, we were just about a month away from the end of the hurricane season when a weather system formed and had it's eyes set not just on our region but directly on our island. In preparation we made plans to have our clients leave the island.

From Leadership to Legacy

A part of my responsibility was to ensure that each client was given a letter upon departure that provided details on steps the company was encouraging them to take, the responsibility the company assumed, and also how the company was going over and above in compensating them for the disruption to their experience. Each client upon checkout was to be met by either myself or my assistant. We had some details to communicate, the letter to provide, and a request for their signature upon receipt of this letter.

That morning things were going smoothly. No one was panicking, well mostly no one as we will soon see otherwise. The clients were not just at ease with how things were being handled, but appreciated the lengths the company went to communicate with them, and ensure they were well taken care of.

As my assistant came in and things slowed down a bit, I briefed my her on how things had been flowing, provided her with the extra copies of the letters and the sheet for the signatures. This was pretty standard for us. Besides, this being company protocol hurricanes and the procedures weren't new to us.

After updating her, I informed her where I would be assisting with other clients who were still trying to leave the island. The rest of my team was informed as well, not just on my location but also that my assistant would be meeting with the departing clients. Within ten minutes of leaving the lobby of the hotel a

What You Say

colleague and friend of mine came rushing in indicating that the top executive was really upset because he was speaking to a couple who was preparing to leave and had not received their letter and that he was asking where I was.

I told my colleague that my assistant had the letters, the team was completely aware of what was happening and who was doing what and that I had just left my assistant standing where she needed to be. My colleague seemed really concerned, a little distressed even, and so I left to see what was happening. Now imagine this walkway that stretched about 150ft. When I turned a corner that was at one end of that walkway, I saw the executive she was talking about, who was also my immediate boss, walking in my direction from the other end. On the top of his lungs with a team member and a guest in earshot he started complaining and then stated that I instilled no confidence.

I have to be honest and still to this day I struggle to think of how I would have handled that differently, but as he continued and approached me I walked right by him, pretty much not acknowledging his existence in that moment and any witnesses would have wondered who he was talking to because nothing about my face or body language even indicated I heard someone speaking let alone speaking to me.

As I walked by him and was about to enter the area I left my assistant standing, the same place I had been all morning, my assistant approached me. I asked her what was going on and if there was in fact a couple that didn't receive a letter. She advised me that she spoke with the couple, they had their letter, and had already signed.

I will save the details on what the conversation was ultimately like when I went to address my boss about what he said, where he said it, and how he said it. We will get into that in a bit.

He was sincerely of the belief that what should have happened didn't happen and that would only give cause to consider how many other times it didn't happen and what the implications could have been. I share this encounter because this is a perfect example of how what you say can create damage with your team and in your team if we aren't mindful.

As a leader myself and having first hand knowledge of why it was critical that all clients were directly communicated with, given the written communication and their signature received, it is not lost on me why any leader would be concerned. However, the words that did not even address the matter at hand were used to express the anger and frustration he was feeling at that moment.

Let's say his anger and frustration were duly warranted, as leaders who have to recognise that even in correcting someone on our team, that correction needs to point them forward not pull them back. The words need to build them up, not tear them down.

What You Say

The words need to guide them and not be used to beat them or cast judgment.

What we say as leaders matter. Our words help to create vision. They shape the buy in and belief of that vision. They also create a clear direction and influence the belief of the team about what is possible for them as a unit and as individuals. Becoming intentional with our words, ensuring that they are crafted with thought and consideration is critical. This is beyond simply being mindful of what you say because of the feelings of others, this is being mindful because you recognise that your words carry weight...weight that impacts outcome.

Someone of a different nature than I had at the time, could have internalised what he said, could have taken that and assigned everything he said as true about themselves and start to shrink, start to play it safe, start to not speak up, start to question their value and what they bring. What is the impact of that kind of thinking beyond that person? When someone starts thinking and seeing themselves this way and they are on your team, what do you think they are going to bring to the team? Do you think they will express their ideas or feel free to share any creative suggestions? Do they come and play full out or are they tucked in the corner doing just enough of what needs to get done? Are they trying to grow and expand their capacity or did they let what was said be what they demonstrate because they believed it?

We would love to believe everyone comes into the workforce fully equipped, ready and willing to not just learn but expand. That isn't always, or dare I say often, the case. Sometimes people come without even a clear view of who they are and who they could be. Many are driven simply because they are drawn to a particular field of interest, but are completely unaware that growth beyond their existing technical ability is even in the realm of possibility. There are also those who feel something else lying dormant inside them, itching to get out, but they don't know what that something is, how they can cultivate it, or even "risk" exploring where it takes them.

A leader who is able to change not just organisations, but is able to change lives, change the way their people see themselves and their capacity for more, seeks to use their words to build even in the toughest circumstances and yes even in critiquing the actions of their team.

When You Say

The right thing at the wrong time is a wrong thing.

Joshua Harris

Has someone ever said something to you and the timing was just wrong. What they said could have been right or helpful, but the timing made you want to look at them and ask, do you have a brain? A sense of conscience maybe? Just a little discretion?

Believe it or not, this is a skill that leaders need if they are going to groom other leaders, impact the growth of an organisation and elevate their people to multiple next level shifts as human beings.

For my skeptics and cynics reading, this does not mean that you are constantly tip-toeing around the feelings of your team, but yes we are engaging emotional intelligence. What's the difference? Using emotional intelligence is a strategy. It's not meant to simply communicate in a way that allows a person to

feel good. Your emotional intelligence can be employed as a strategy that helps you use successful methods to impact your people as individuals.

Take this time I had a team member who had just gone through a disciplinary matter. The company policy dictated that the next time he returned to work, there should be a meeting with me as his leader before he re-engaged in the workplace. Well on the day he was scheduled to return, I got a call at work from his family. His father had passed away and they weren't able to reach him. Even greater, they had a concern for how he would take the news and that he was on a small island away from everyone and were curious how they could get him to return to his city without having actual knowledge before arriving.

I won't go into all the details, but I helped them and got him on a flight to head home. At the time all he knew for sure was that his father was not well and he needed to go home.

When he did return to work, which happened to be before the memorial service, the nature of my conversation was different than it would have been if he did not have that experience. I know some may not agree but I can only speak to the things that helped me that I know impacted the teams I led and the results they produced. He was going to be heading back off in a few days for his father's service so at that point I wanted to do a check-in. Extend some empathy and support. Assess if he was in fact in a frame of mind that was conducive for work and let him know that I had an open door, a listening ear and was available.

When he returned from the additional time away to attend the service, I still did a check-in. Towards the end of that meeting I briefly revisited the matter that had led to his suspension and we agreed on what the focus needed to be to ensure there wasn't a repeat. While I took the time to recap what happened, why it was a breach and reiterated the expectations moving forward, I was also sure to reassure him that I was there to support him.

The company's guidelines directed leaders to meet with any person on the team that was temporarily excused from the operation for disciplinary matters upon their return. However, after consulting with Human Resources, I delayed that conversation given the circumstances. I thought it was best to delay that conversation.

As a leader, wisdom is critical to the process of building connection and creating impact. I could have absolutely met with him and had that conversation upon his initial return, but he was likely not to really hear me. He was likely to feel additional pressure and perceive a lack of empathy. Weighing those things against what was happening in the operation and what he would be doing in the 3 days he would be on the job before leaving for the memorial service, having that conversation and the potential ramifications, I believed it more beneficial to delay.

I am not proposing that leaders not speak, not correct and not communicate. What I am saying is that within the guidelines of company policy, timing is also an element you must pay attention to. Handling corrective feedback in front of other members of the team, in front of clients, or when you as the leader have not checked your own emotions at the door is unwise and very damaging.

How You Say

The tone is the message.

Kevin T McCarney

I'm sure you have been there. You know the kind of experience when someone said something to you and you can't even hear the message because of how it was said. You are stuck replaying their words in your head and instead of hearing the words all you keep hearing is the tone their voice had. It may have been strained with condescension, held a hint of sarcasm or laced with hurt or anger.

Leaders not only take ownership of what they say but how they say it. They recognise that more important than what comes out of their mouths is the impact of those words. As a result, leaders are intentional in how they communicate what they have to say.

Communicating in a way that increases resistance to receiving the information is something leaders know is one of the most unproductive things they can do. Maintaining a high level of intention in how you communicate takes work and time to build, particularly when faced with difficult, unpleasant, or emergency circumstances.

Communication should always be used to inform, build, encourage, and to move systems, projects, and results forward. A strong leader is unwilling to continuously communicate in a way that does the opposite. They also know that the more often communication is flawed, the more productivity is affected.

This is an area that far too many decision makers are dismissive of. Many often mistakenly believe that their teams ought to just focus on the information being communicated and dismiss the tone. This is a very damaging mistake. You may have the experience of someone being on your team that may not be as impacted just by the nature of their personality. However, you are still sending them a message about who you are and how you view them. Many of your people however, are unlikely to be that dismissive. Your tone is a part of the message. To ignore this simple fact is to ignore the implications of sending a damaging message that affects results.

When you are the decision maker leading a team of people, the responsibility of initiating, facilitating, and maintaining effective communication is firstly your responsibility.

Void of this intentional approach to communication, decision makers can alienate team members, block communication all together, erode the respect and cooperation they garner from their team and also seriously erode their ability to influence, impact and build connection with their team.

Let's go back to the example I gave two chapters ago. You know, the one where I was told I instill no confidence? Yeah, that one. Let's for a moment disregard where we were, what was happening and the fact that the immediate focus should have been on resolving whatever the issue was. I can even overlook the choice of words. Sure even when communicated in a professional tone, those words have a certain sting to them.

However, how it was said, the volume and the tone, really communicated in that moment someone who was just fed up and frustrated and was quite frankly unconcerned about communicating for the purpose of arriving at a resolution or effecting change. The sentiment came as a surprise to me, not because I felt I was perfect, but because there was never any communication previously that suggested this.

Listen, we are all human, we all have areas that we can build on and become better in. That's just a statement of fact. For a moment, let us disregard the other elements that did not portray him well that day and examine the following:

- Does communicating this way help or hurt the

ability to achieve the desired result?

- Does how I communicate foster mutual respect?

- Does how I communicate reflect that I have the interest of my team at heart?

- Does the manner and nature in which I communicate reflect the way I want to be communicated with?

Again, this may take a great deal of self awareness and effort for most, but it is necessary. I also can't emphasize the need to take ownership for the moments you recognise you fell short in this area.

My own leadership journey had moments where the manner in which I communicated was not the way it should have been. While thankfully, these moments were not excessive and my journey isn't overrun with them, I have been frustrated and communicated with less patience or calm than I should have. What has always, ALWAYS, benefitted me is that I quickly take ownership. Taking ownership as a leader in those circumstances, for me, meant that I stood by what was said but apologised for the less than effective way it was communicated. I am able to do that because of the level of self-awareness I have developed and continue to.

How You Say

Developing that level of awareness, recognising any time I failed myself or my team in how I communicated and taking ownership of that is one of the reasons that I was able to garner trust and respect the way I was from my teams. I was demonstrating to them that I held myself accountable just as I do them. They understood that I had respect for them when I apologised when it was right to do so.

Many decision makers are afraid of operating in this level of transparency because they are seeking power. Truth is, in my experience, the more your team recognises that you operate in integrity, take ownership, are invested in their development and want to see them win, they will give you their loyalty, their best effort and do for you because of you and not because of your title. That beats trying to attain power through intimidation, fear and bullying any day.

The manner in which you communicate is speaking just as loudly as your actual words.

Connection

Invest

Management is about arranging and telling. Leadership is about nurturing & enhancing.

Tom Peter's

A lot of people with the responsibility of guiding others to a goal make some critical mistakes. I know because I have made my own as well and had to learn from them. One of the mistakes that was not my own, but that I've witnessed is the lack of investing in their teams.

A quick search for the definition of investment gave me:

1. **refer to any mechanism used for generating future income.**

2. **to make use of for future benefits or advantages**

3. **to involve or engage especially emotionally**

So then, what is the mistake that is being made? Leaders are literally overlooking, bypassing, undervaluing or even completely ignoring the concept of investing in their teams. They ignore the concept of making use of their team for future benefit, advantage, and income.

Let's break this thing down like four flat tires. Investing is going to require that you take something of value, in this case your time, your knowledge, your experience and engage your team, deposit it in them for the purpose of benefiting in the future.

What are you investing? It is more than just your time. It is your knowledge, your experience and what those two things have developed in you. Yes absolutely from a technical perspective, but even more importantly investing your efforts to engage and build their critical thinking, their emotional intelligence, their ability to cast vision for a team and for themselves and most importantly teaching them leadership including self leadership. You invest in them by training, observing, listening to and providing feedback for their progress that goes beyond the typical performance review conversations.

It is simply powerful to think of a leader who is so grounded that they are perfectly in tune with the continuous reward of having a team that is having leadership modeled for them, taught to them and groomed in them. That long before any of them may even step into an assigned role that calls for them to lead well, they already stand so certain in who they are, what they bring,

Invest

how they contribute and how they themselves lead and effect change and growth.

Who benefits? They benefit because they have more knowledge that equips them to do more, be more effective and efficient, take more ownership, problem solve with greater ease and all this improves the value they offer to the organisation and that helps them to be positioned for growth.

You benefit. Your job literally becomes easier. How? You are not the only one operating with the knowledge that you have when you learn to pour, or invest, that knowledge into your team. SO...the level of decision making and execution improves tremendously. You now have people who are more equipped, whose capacity is being stretched, who are literally being taught what you know. They accomplish more and you benefit more because you have a team that is more effective and delivers beyond just what their experience alone would enable them to deliver.

Finally the organisation benefits from having an increased number of people operating more effectively in their zones of genius and who are also becoming leaders in their own right.

Allow me to introduce you to a young lady that worked with me. We affectionately call her TC. When TC was first recruited on my team, she had little to no experience for the area she was hired for. In fact, it was a brand new department being established at that location that I was tasked with getting up and running. I had to recruit, train, handle decisions regarding how the physical infrastructure would support the work they needed to do, source uniforms since the organisation wouldn't be able to supply them quickly enough, and a host of other things. TC was among the first group recruited and went through an intense training program meant to equip them in a very short space of time. It was clear that she was someone that I would have to invest a lot of effort to groom and build for the role, but her willingness was unmatched and I took a chance on her.

Staged in the same location I referenced before with a small population and an even more devastatingly small workforce, the reality that TC's first interview did not present her as the ideal candidate but her willingness and eagerness to learn was to her advantage.

After a short while, it was evident that her willingness and humility exceeded what she believed she had the capacity to deliver in execution. Despite my best efforts to train, follow up, coach, guide, suggest and the works, TC's performance proved to be developing at the absolute best. The frustrating part was I saw that she was capable of more than she was providing. However, it came to the point where I had to make the decision to release her from employment after keeping her as long as I could have and pouring as much into her as was humanly possible in the time we had. Let's just say her attitude coerced a lot of grace out of me and so did our unique set of manning challenges. Her exit meeting and interview was, to date, one of the most disappointing for me because her approach, attitude and personality were all a leader's dream. Her execution would then be, well, a nightmare.

A little over a year after being released, while I was still in the deep waters of being woefully under my manning, TC reached out to me. She was upfront in explaining why she was requesting an opportunity to speak with me. She wanted another chance at the job but politely asked me for an opportunity to share some things. When we spoke she mentioned that she had a lot of time to reflect. She spoke about how much she disappointed herself looking back at her performance when she was with the team. She mentioned that during her time with us, she felt like she was giving it her best effort but, as hindsight is perfect, she recognised that was not the case. She not only acknowledged the shortcomings she displayed but she took complete ownership. It was evident that this wasn't her trying to impress me simply to get her job back. She really was disappointed in her previous performance and seemed to have a score to settle with herself. We had a need on the team for more people. So after reestablishing what I would be expecting and that my grace wouldn't be as pronounced this time around, she successfully rejoined the team.

TC got right to work. She was committed, learning, applying and delivering even beyond what I had initially seen in her. Within two years she had been the recipient of multiple award nominations. She was the only team member in over 600 people to receive a 100% rating on three separate secret shopper reports over the course of 16 months. TC was doing so well that in 2 years we started really focusing on what was next for her in terms of the path she truly wanted her career to take. I had known that her ambitions didn't include the department she was working in. It had always been a stage in the process she was taking to lead her where she wanted to go.

I coached her through the process of starting to position herself for the job she wanted next, in the area she truly desired. She had already done such an excellent job in her area, established her value, voice, and vision and solidified her visibility. When she applied for the role she had been eyeing, the value she could bring to the role was already evident. She stepped into that role confidently and continued conquering one role after the next in that area. If there ever was a comeback story, TC was it.

After I left corporate, TC spent some time working with me in my coaching program and by the end of her 3 months with me, she started her own financial services business.

Invest

When leaders invest in their people, the benefit goes far beyond the vision for what organisational objectives are. You are helping develop someone. You are sharing all you know, you are literally pouring into them every single resource you can to help them and equipping them to perform, to grow and to excel.

Leaders shift into legacy when they release any insecurity about sharing all they know to support effectiveness, efficiency and growth. Leaders who make the kind of impact that mobilises people to pursue greater and become more are not threatened. In fact they realise everyone stands to gain when people are supported in operating in their zone of genius.

Support

"If your actions inspire others to dream more, learn more, do more and become more, you are a leader."

John Quincy Adams

So when you are building connection, the support you offer to your team is a fundamental part of that process. Building connection comes through building trust and aside from operating with integrity, support, which is defined as the ability to enable to function or act, is a part of the foundation.

Think about your own life, likely some of the people that you have the greatest connection with are people who you trust. You trust them because they have proven themselves as trustworthy and have also proven that their intentions towards you are good.

In the context of leadership, your ability to exhibit trustworthiness in your intentions for your team is directly associated with how you enable them to function or act. Your team is going to consciously or unconsciously be scrutinizing how you equip them, which has to do with training and all that is done to provide them with the information they need to apply. The support is now the application process, how you are guiding them through the mistakes, the success, the setback and the wins.

It is not sufficient to simply give them the information and tools. To build connection they will need to see that you are also invested in how they show up, how they apply what has been poured into them, and to guide them through the different obstacles and hurdles that they may not have even known to anticipate.

A manager who provides training and then backs off and expects everyone to just fall in line, do what needs to be done and does not engage in the part of the process that comes after the training and investing of information, is setting themselves and their teams up for failure or best case scenario for limited success.

Consider what your team perceives. While people come into organisations with different expectations and needs, there is something unlocked in a person when they recognise you, as the leader, are committed to not just giving them what they should have and equipping them from a technical perspective but that you have a concern that as they are growing in their roles, you are investing in and supporting them in growing in their execution and supporting them grow as people.

Support

No one would go to a goldmine and just take what was at the entrance or what was on the surface. They keep digging and keep panning because what is on the surface is only the beginning, but you have to work to be able to recover the rest. The people on your team are like these goldmines. Sure you could stop when you first uncover the presence of gold, but then you are leaving so much value covered and unprofitable just sitting there.

People want to be seen and valued. Being seen is not the same as making a fuss about and always being applauded before others. I am not necessarily speaking about that. I am speaking about seeing your team as individuals, not as employee number 9294. See who they are, the value they offer and their capacity for more. Also see who they can become and how all of that can align with the goals of the organisation and also support them in actualizing who they desire to be.

Now before you start rolling your eyes again, hear me out. Yes, your team individually also has a responsibility to themselves, their future, their growth and their success. What I am saying is you will have amazing people on your team that:

1. Are blind to their own potential and capacity. The same untapped potential and capacity that will be beneficial to the organisation if harnessed.

2. Have the awareness that there is more in them but

are not equipped to navigate the industry and the responsibilities as a leader. So to be able to fully develop having a leader who is committed to guiding them through that part of the journey is going to be rewarding for all involved on multiple levels.

What is most crucial in this phase when you are supporting, is knowing that you will witness your people have wins and also make mistakes. As a leader that is offering support, this requires you to build, not demolish when a mistake is made. What do I mean? Let's say someone on your team, that you have offered the training to, you have been monitoring, communicating and guiding but as is inevitable, makes a mistake. Your correction should be building them, teaching them how to avoid that in the future even if you know they could have and should have avoided that mistake.

I don't know how common it is but I suspect it is not very common. I have had the good fortune on multiple occasions over the course of my 19 years in corporate to be seated in meetings where I am having to correct behaviours or in some cases release people from employment. While some ended with the expected awkwardness or disappointment I have had more that have ended with them thanking me for all I have helped them to grow into, what I helped them learn about themselves, what is possible for them and for my support. I wish someone

Support

would give me money for each time I was told "thank you for seeing in me what I didn't see in myself."

A huge part of that is what we are about to dive into in the next chapter but also a large part of this was because I didn't just leave them to their own devices. I was constantly monitoring, assessing, communicating, teaching, training, tweaking and guiding. Whatever the disciplinary process is within your organisation, as a leader your sense of helping to hold your team accountable cannot be solely reliant on that process. There should be an inner nudge and desire to be able to help your people make the connection between the principles and technical skills they have learned and the actual application and increased effectiveness and efficiency in that application.

As a child your mother or father would have said to you one day to put on a pair of pants. Before this happened it is something they would have been demonstrating to you each time they did it for you, before you got to the stage where they recognised you should be capable of doing it yourself. After that stage they would likely start calling your attention to how it was done and allowing you to do it in their presence. They would recognise the challenge you had and taught you simple ways that you could do it more effectively. Soon you were getting yourself dressed, but when they would come to your room what would they be doing? Giving you a quick glance to ensure you did it properly.

Checking that your clothes were put on correctly and in place.

All throughout that process the support was evident. You were not just left to figure it out and walk out of your home with the zipper in the back and your underwear showing. No. There was a steady progression of giving you more and more room, trust, and independence. This is leadership support.

Challenge

A leader will consistently challenge you to grow, expand your capacity, be more and see more for yourself.

Marsha Flemmings

A few years into my career, I had the experience of working with an immediate boss, who was in my opinion, a master at challenging his team. This concept of challenge says that you never create an atmosphere that allows your team, individually and collectively to become complacent. A lot of people saw his approach as micromanaging. What he was doing, at least in my experience with him, was not that.

I was a young leader and I meant well, was hardworking, and driven. He was a senior executive who also had a lot more experience in the industry. What was most impactful to me was how he challenged me. My team and I were doing well. We had come up with new ideas and implemented them all. I groomed the team so well that our effectiveness and efficiency increased significantly and it showed in the key performance indicators. We weren't perfect in every single area, but we were doing a great job and getting better. Whenever we would launch a new idea or get to another level of performance, he always challenged me with, "so what's next?"

He consistently acknowledged any progress we had made, but he would never allow me to rest on the last accomplishment. The question was always the same. So what's next?

This usually caused me to assess each area of my operation looking for any possible deficiencies and also looking for opportunities to improve on what we were doing well. Now I had recognised that I had an internal tracking system that would always allow me to start feeling very unsettled when I had offered all I could give to one role, one team, or organisation. The trouble is that I got a season where what I initially wanted for my career was starting to change. I had already accomplished some of it and was still growing, but this change in desire made his usual question perplexing because when directed at me specifically I wasn't sure what was next. I ultimately had to do the heavy lifting by answering this question, but some of my conversations with him really kept me in a deep introspective mode.

A leader, even in the midst of great accomplishment, will celebrate you, they will help you identify what really got you to

Challenge

where you are, but will challenge you to look at what is next and how you get there.

So the question then becomes are you that leader to your team?

We have the power, no, the opportunity to be a part of the work that these individuals and groups produce in this world, helping them make it better and helping to make them better. That's when we shift from leadership to legacy.

Epilogue

You made it! You stuck with me through this journey and by now you have a clear vision. You know exactly how to build synergy within your team. You know what it takes to build trust that creates opportunity to influence and you understand and appreciate how this fuels your success, the success of your team and organisation.

There is no time to waste. You can't afford to create any further delay in your approach to grooming and growing your team as that has a direct influence on how your organisation grows. While this investment requires a long term view, being willing to build connection and trust will yield a more engaged, better equipped, confident, and growing team that makes achieving your company's goals that much easier. You ultimately build a reputation of building high performing teams and creating other leaders.

Let's take a quick look at what we covered and what you will now implement to create change, growth and impact within your team.

Chapter 1 - Create a clearly defined vision of the type of leader you will be. How you communicate, how you show up, how you engage, how you adapt to change, how you handle conflict, and how you challenge and support your team.

Chapter 2 - You created a vision for the goals you and your team will accomplish.

Chapter 3 - You created a vision for your team. If people are following you, they want to know where you are taking them. So what is the vision for how your team will communicate, grow, and work to their strengths? You learned how to ensure you have your players positioned properly and how to keep guiding them to growth and stretching their capacity.

Chapter 4 - You are able to differentiate between your internal view of yourself and the view others have of you.

Chapter 5 - Without the ability to see yourself, know your triggers, motivators and response in both kinds of situations you will be operating with blindspots that are affecting your results and effectiveness as a leader.

Chapter 6- We spoke about what you communicate verbally and non verbally. Leaders take ownership of the impact of their words and do not speak carelessly.

Epilogue

Chapter 7 - You recognise that timing of what you communicate is also essential. Delay in communicating critical information impacts results. We also examined the importance of acknowledging a job well done, improved effort and initiative is also just as important as corrective feedback. Your voice should not only be heard in performance reviews.

Chapter 8 - At the very core of leadership is the ability to guide others to a particular set of outcomes. It will be difficult to do so effectively if how you communicate generally creates a disconnect. Communication of vision, direction, correction and praise should be consistently practiced. Repetition reinforces learning.

Chapter 9 - Leaders equip their teams, not just with tools but also with the information they need to not just do well but excel.

Chapter 10 - Leaders who succeed understand that supporting your team is not just offering praise, but knowing how to correct

Chapter 11 - Successful leaders challenge their teams to keep growing, to avoid complacency and stagnation

www.ingramcontent.com/pod-product-compliance
Lightning Source LLC
Chambersburg PA
CBHW070133100426
42744CB00009B/1821